TRANZLATY

Lingua est pro omnibus

Language is for everyone

Pulchritudo et Bestia

Beauty and the Beast

Gabrielle-Suzanne Barbot de Villeneuve

Latin / English

Copyright © 2025 Tranzlaty
All rights reserved
Published by Tranzlaty
ISBN: 978-1-83566-980-8
Original text by Gabrielle-Suzanne Barbot de Villeneuve
La Belle et la Bête
First published in French in 1740
Taken from The Blue Fairy Book (Andrew Lang)
Illustration by Walter Crane
www.tranzlaty.com

Fuit aliquando dives mercator
There was once a rich merchant
dives mercator sex liberos
this rich merchant had six children
habuit tres filios et tres filias
he had three sons and three daughters
non pepercit sumptibus educationis
he spared no cost for their education
quia vir sensus erat
because he was a man of sense
sed liberis servis multos dedit
but he gave his children many servants
eius filiae sunt maxime pulchra
his daughters were extremely pretty
et filia eius minima erat maxime pulchra
and his youngest daughter was especially pretty
sicut puer eius pulchritudinem iam admiratus
as a child her Beauty was already admired
et vocavit eam populus a facie sua
and the people called her by her Beauty
eius pulchritudo non veterascet cum illa got maior
her Beauty did not fade as she got older
et vocabat eam populus a facie sua
so the people kept calling her by her Beauty
hoc fecit ei sororibus valde zelotypus
this made her sisters very jealous
duabus filiabus natu plurimum superbiae
the two eldest daughters had a great deal of pride
opes eorum fons superbiae
their wealth was the source of their pride
et non absconderunt superbiam suam
and they didn't hide their pride either
alias filias mercatorum non visitaverunt
they did not visit other merchants' daughters
quia nonnisi ad aristocratiam
because they only meet with aristocracy

partes exierunt cotidie
they went out every day to parties
pilae, fabulae, concentus, salutem
balls, plays, concerts, and so forth
et deridebant ad minorem sororem suam
and they laughed at their youngest sister
propter eam maximam sui temporis legere
because she spent most of her time reading
notum erat quod divites
it was well known that they were wealthy
ideo plures nobiles mercatores pro manu sua petierunt
so several eminent merchants asked for their hand
sed dixerunt se non nupturam
but they said they were not going to marry
sed parati erant aliqua exceptione facere
but they were prepared to make some exceptions
"Ducere fortasse potui"
"perhaps I could marry a Duke"
"Ego coniecto potui ducere comiti"
"I guess I could marry an Earl"
pulchritudo valde civiliter gratias illis quae proponuntur ei
Beauty very civilly thanked those that proposed to her
non indicavit eis adhuc minor nubere
she told them she was still too young to marry
voluit manere aliquot annos cum patre suo
she wanted to stay a few more years with her father

Statim mercator suam fortunam perdidit
All at once the merchant lost his fortune
amisit omnia sine parva villa
he lost everything apart from a small country house
et flens in oculis suis dixit:
and he told his children with tears in his eyes:
"ire eundum est ad villam"
"we must go to the countryside"
"et nobis viventibus opus est".

"and we must work for our living"
duabus filiabus natu maximis nolebat decedere oppido
the two eldest daughters didn't want to leave the town
plures in urbe habebant
they had several lovers in the city
et erant quidam amantes eorum se nubant
and they were sure one of their lovers would marry them
amantes etiam nulla fortuna nubere eos putabant
they thought their lovers would marry them even with no fortune
sed erraverunt bonae dominae
but the good ladies were mistaken
amantes dereliquerunt celerrime
their lovers abandoned them very quickly
quia nullae erant amplius fortunae
because they had no fortunes any more
hoc ostendit se non esse bene probaverunt
this showed they were not actually well liked
omnes dixerunt non esse miserendum
everybody said they do not deserve to be pitied
"Laetamur humilem videre superbiam".
"we are glad to see their pride humbled"
"Sint superbi vaccarum vaccarum"
"let them be proud of milking cows"
sed ad pulchritudinem
but they were concerned for Beauty
fuit tam dulcis creatura
she was such a sweet creature
et locutus est ad populum pauperem misericordiam
she spoke so kindly to poor people
et erat talis innocens
and she was of such an innocent nature
Plures nobiles eam uxorem habuisset
Several gentlemen would have married her
matrimonio iuncti essent eam etsi pauper erat
they would have married her even though she was poor

sed dixit eis se non posse ducere
but she told them she couldn't marry them
quia noluit patrem suum relinquere
because she would not leave her father
quæ voluit ire cum eo in villam
she was determined to go with him to the countryside
ut eum consolari posset et adiuvare
so that she could comfort and help him

Misera forma valde contristatus est primo
Poor Beauty was very grieved at first
illa amissione fortunae doluit
she was grieved by the loss of her fortune
" sed lacrimans fortunas meas non mutabit "
"but crying won't change my fortunes"
"Conabor sine divitiis me beatum facere"
"I must try to make myself happy without wealth"
venerunt in villam suam
they came to their country house
et mercator cum tribus filiis agriculturae operam dabant
and the merchant and his three sons applied themselves to husbandry
pulchritudinis quattuor mane
Beauty rose at four in the morning
et festinavit mundare domum
and she hurried to clean the house
et certa cena parata erat
and she made sure dinner was ready
in principio invenit eam novam vitam difficillimam
in the beginning she found her new life very difficult
quia non fuerat usus tali opere
because she had not been used to such work
sed minus quam duobus mensibus ipsa convalescit
but in less than two months she grew stronger
et salubrius fuit
and she was healthier than ever before

postquam factum est opus eius quae legit
after she had done her work she read
illa quatientes citharista
she played on the harpsichord
aut canebat dum fila sericum
or she sung whilst she spun silk
sed duae sorores eius nesciverunt tempus terere
on the contrary, her two sisters did not know how to spend their time
surgentes decem et nihil aliud quam otiosi dies
they got up at ten and did nothing but laze about all day
amissa veste gemebant
they lamented the loss of their fine clothes
et de amissis notis conquesti sunt
and they complained about losing their acquaintances
"Inspice sororem nostram minimissimam"
"Have a look at our youngest sister," they said to each other
" quam pauper et stultus creatura est "
"what a poor and stupid creature she is"
"Est tantillo contentum esse"
"it is mean to be content with so little"
Mercator longe alia sententia fuit
the kind merchant was of quite a different opinion
bene sciebat illam pulchritudinem sororibus praelucere
he knew very well that Beauty outshone her sisters
illa praelucebat in mores tum mentis
she outshone them in character as well as mind
humilitatem eius et laborem
he admired her humility and her hard work
sed maxime miratus est eius patientiam
but most of all he admired her patience
sororibus eius relinquentes eam omne opus facere
her sisters left her all the work to do
et insultaverunt ei omni tempore
and they insulted her every moment

Familia sic per annum circiter vixerat
The family had lived like this for about a year
deinde mercator litteras de tabulario accepit
then the merchant got a letter from an accountant
habuit obsidendi in navi
he had an investment in a ship
et navis tuto advenit
and the ship had safely arrived
t eius nuntium convertit capita duarum natu maximarum
this news turned the heads of the two eldest daughters
spem redeundi in oppidum statim habebant
they immediately had hopes of returning to town
quia pertaesi erant
because they were quite weary of country life
digredientem ad patrem
they went to their father as he was leaving
orabant ut novas vestes emeret
they begged him to buy them new clothes
coquit, vittas et omnium rerum parvarum
dresses, ribbons, and all sorts of little things
sed pulchritudo poposcit nihil
but Beauty asked for nothing
quia putavit pecuniam non satis esse
because she thought the money wasn't going to be enough
satis non esset emere omnia sororibus suis voluerunt
there wouldn't be enough to buy everything her sisters wanted
"Quid vis, pulchritudo?" interrogavit pater eius
"What would you like, Beauty?" asked her father
"gratias tibi, pater, pro bonitate cogitare de me"
"thank you, father, for the goodness to think of me," she said
"Pater mi, sis dignare ut rosam afferat".
"father, be so kind as to bring me a rose"
"quia nullae rosae hic nascuntur in horto"
"because no roses grow here in the garden"
"rosae sunt quaedam raritas".

"and roses are a kind of rarity"
pulchritudo non vere curare ut rosis
Beauty didn't really care for roses
non solum aliquid poposcit, ut sorores eius non condemnent
she only asked for something not to condemn her sisters
Sorores autem eius videbantur aliis de causis rosas poposcit
but her sisters thought she asked for roses for other reasons
"Hoc fecit solum spectare maxime"
"she did it just to look particular"

Homo quidam iter fecit
The kind man went on his journey
sed cum venisset, de mercibus disputaverunt
but when he arrived they argued about the merchandise
et post multam molestiam egens rediit sicut prius
and after a lot of trouble he came back as poor as before
fuit intra horas domus suae
he was within a couple of hours of his own house
et iam laetitiam videndi suorum
and he already imagined the joy of seeing his children
sed cum per silvas amisisset
but when going through forest he got lost
pluit ac ninxit terribly
it rained and snowed terribly
adeo vehemens ventus proiecit equo
the wind was so strong it threw him off his horse
et nox cito veniebat
and night was coming quickly
cogitare coepit ut esuriret
he began to think that he might starve
et ad mortem se duraturum arbitrabatur
and he thought that he might freeze to death
et putabat lupi comedendum eum
and he thought wolves may eat him
luporum audisse circum se ululantes
the wolves that he heard howling all round him

sed subito vidit lucem
but all of a sudden he saw a light
lucem procul vidit per arbores
he saw the light at a distance through the trees
ubi propius accedens lucem vidit palatium;
when he got closer he saw the light was a palace
palatium a summo usque deorsum
the palace was illuminated from top to bottom
mercator Deo gratias pro sua fortuna
the merchant thanked God for his luck
et festinavit ad palatium
and he hurried to the palace
sed miratus est nullum homines videre in palatio
but he was surprised to see no people in the palace
atrium vacuum erat
the court yard was completely empty
et signum vitae nusquam erat
and there was no sign of life anywhere
eum secutus est equus in regiam
his horse followed him into the palace
et invenit equum magnum stabulum
and then his horse found large stable
pauper animal paene famelicus
the poor animal was almost famished
Et ingressus est equus ad inveniendum fenum et avenam
so his horse went in to find hay and oats
feliciter invenit multa manducare
fortunately he found plenty to eat
et mercator equum suum ad presepe alligavit
and the merchant tied his horse up to the manger
w alking in domo vidit neminem
walking towards the house he saw no one
sed in aula magna invenit ignem bonum
but in a large hall he found a good fire
et invenit mensam unam
and he found a table set for one

erat umidus a pluvia et nivis
he was wet from the rain and snow
Accessit ad ignem siccum
so he went near the fire to dry himself
" Spero patremfamilias excusaturum " ;
"I hope the master of the house will excuse me"
"Puto non diu aliquem apparere"
"I suppose it won't take long for someone to appear"
Diu expectavit
He waited a considerable time
expectavit donec percussit undecim, et nullus venit
he waited until it struck eleven, and still nobody came
tandem adeo esuriit ut diutius expectare non possit
at last he was so hungry that he could wait no longer
Tulitque pullum et comedit eum in duobus offis
he took some chicken and ate it in two mouthfuls
et tremens dum comederet panem
he was trembling while eating the food
post haec pauca vini potiones bibit
after this he drank a few glasses of wine
invalescens animosior exivit de aula
growing more courageous he went out of the hall
et per aliquot magnas atria lustravit
and he crossed through several grand halls
ambulavit per palatium, donec veniret in cubiculum
he walked through the palace until he came into a chamber
thalamum quod habebat in eo stratum magnum valde bonum
a chamber which had an exceeding good bed in it
valde fatigatus ab experimento
he was very much fatigued from his ordeal
tempusque iam noctis
and the time was already past midnight
statuit optimum ostio occludere
so he decided it was best to shut the door
et se cubitum ire arbitratus est

and he concluded he should go to bed

Decem mane erat cum mercator expergefactus
It was ten in the morning when the merchant woke up
sicut cum iret ad resurrectionem, vidit aliquid;
just as he was going to rise he saw something
miratus est veste mutata videre
he was astonished to see a clean set of clothes
in loco ubi sordidis vestibus
in the place where he had left his dirty clothes
certe palatium hoc ad quamdam mediocris pertinet.
"certainly this palace belongs to some kind fairy"
" mediocris qui vidit et misertus est " .
"a fairy who has seen and pitied me"
respexit per fenestram
he looked through a window
sed pro nivis hortum amoenissimum vidit
but instead of snow he saw the most delightful garden
et in horto erant pulcherrimae rosae
and in the garden were the most beautiful roses
Et reversus est ad magnum aulam
he then returned to the great hall
praetorium ubi elit nocte
the hall where he had had soup the night before
et invenit scelerisque aliquam parvam mensam
and he found some chocolate on a little table
"Gratias tibi ago, bone Madam Fairy", clara voce dixit
"Thank you, good Madam Fairy," he said aloud
"Gratias ago tibi, quia non ita curans"
"thank you for being so caring"
" Gratissimum tibi sum pro omnibus tuis beneficiis "
"I am extremely obliged to you for all your favours"
genus bibit scelerisque
the kind man drank his chocolate
et ibat ad quaerendum equum suum
and then he went to look for his horse

sed in horto recordatus est petitionem pulchritudinis
but in the garden he remembered Beauty's request
et abscidit ramum rosae
and he cut off a branch of roses
statim audivit clamorem magnum
immediately he heard a great noise
et vidit bestiam horrendam
and he saw a terribly frightful Beast
adeo perterritus erat ut deficeret
he was so scared that he was ready to faint
"Ingratus es," inquit bestia
"You are very ungrateful," said the Beast to him
et bestia voce magna locutus est
and the Beast spoke in a terrible voice
" Servavi vitam tuam permittens te in castrum meum " .
"I have saved your life by allowing you into my castle"
"et pro quo meas surripis rosas?"
"and for this you steal my roses in return?"
"Rosas quas ego pluris aestimo"
"The roses which I value beyond anything"
"sed morieris quod feceris"
"but you shall die for what you've done"
"Ego tibi do, sed quadrantem horae para te";
"I give you but a quarter of an hour to prepare yourself"
"paratus te ad mortem et dic preces tuas"
"get yourself ready for death and say your prayers"
mercator ad genua procumbit
the merchant fell on his knees
et levavit ambas manus suas
and he lifted up both his hands
Obsecro te, domine mi, ut indulgeas mihi.
"My lord, I beseech you to forgive me"
"Nihil habui animus tibi offensionis"
"I had no intention of offending you"
Rosam congregavi uni filiarum mearum.
"I gathered a rose for one of my daughters"

" **Rogavit me ut rosam adduceret** "
"she asked me to bring her a rose"
"**monstrum**" respondit "**Non sum dominus tuus, sed bestia**
"I am not your lord, but I am a Beast," replied the monster
"**Non amo verborum**"
"I don't love compliments"
" **Placet illis qui loquuntur sicut cogitant** ";
"I like people who speak as they think"
"**ne putes me blanditiis posse moveri**".
"do not imagine I can be moved by flattery"
"**At dices filias te peperisse**";
"But you say you have got daughters"
"**Dimitto tibi in una conditione**".
"I will forgive you on one condition"
"**una filiarum tuarum libenter in palatium meum venire debet**".
"one of your daughters must come to my palace willingly"
"**et debet pati pro vobis**".
"and she must suffer for you"
" **Fiat mihi verbum tuum** "
"Let me have your word"
"**Et tunc potes ire de negotiis tuis**"
"and then you can go about your business"
"**Hoc mihi promitte;**"
"Promise me this:"
"**Si filia tua pro te mori noluerit, intra tres menses redibis**".
"if your daughter refuses to die for you, you must return within three months"
mercator non habuit filias suas sacrificare
the merchant had no intentions to sacrifice his daughters
sed, cum tempus daretur, filias suas denuo videre voluit
but, since he was given time, he wanted to see his daughters once more
Itaque se rediturum pollicitus est
so he promised he would return
et dixit ei bestia, quam vellet, proficisci

and the Beast told him he might set out when he pleased
et bestia indicavit ei unum amplius
and the Beast told him one more thing
"non recedes inanis"
"you shall not depart empty handed"
"Ire ad cubiculum ubi iaces"
"go back to the room where you lay"
" magnum pectus thesaurum inane videbis "
"you will see a great empty treasure chest"
"Replete thesaurum, cum quidquid tibi placet optimum"
"fill the treasure chest with whatever you like best"
"et cistam thesaurum mittam in domum tuam".
"and I will send the treasure chest to your home"
et simul bestia recessit
and at the same time the Beast withdrew

"Bene," dixit sibi vir bonus
"Well," said the good man to himself
"si moriar, liberis meis aliquid saltem relinquam".
"if I must die, I shall at least leave something to my children"
itaque ad cubiculum rediit
so he returned to the bedchamber
invenitque multos aureos
and he found a great many pieces of gold
cistam implevit bestia, de qua dixerat
he filled the treasure chest the Beast had mentioned
et eduxit equum de stabulo
and he took his horse out of the stable
laetitiam, quam in regiam ferebant, moerore relinquendo par erat
the joy he felt when entering the palace was now equal to the grief he felt leaving it
Equus unam viae silvarum
the horse took one of the roads of the forest
et paucis horis bonus domi
and in a few hours the good man was home

filii eius
his children came to him
sed pro libenter amplexus eorum aspexit
but instead of receiving their embraces with pleasure, he looked at them
ramum quem in manibus habebat
he held up the branch he had in his hands
et lacrimas
and then he burst into tears
"pulchritudo" inquit "his rosis sume quaeso"
"Beauty," he said, "please take these roses"
"non scis quam pretiosae fuerint hae rosae"
"you can't know how costly these roses have been"
"Hae rosae patri tuo vitam constant".
"these roses have cost your father his life"
et tunc dixit casus sui fatalis
and then he told of his fatal adventure
Confestim duabus sororibus suis exclamavit
immediately the two eldest sisters cried out
et dixerunt multa media ad pulcherrimam sororem
and they said many mean things to their beautiful sister
sed pulchritudo omnino non clamabit
but Beauty did not cry at all
"Aspice, inquit, illius miselli fastum"
"Look at the pride of that little wretch," said they
"Non quaesivit vestem splendidam"
"she did not ask for fine clothes"
"Debuimus facere quod fecimus"
"she should have done what we did"
"se voluit distinguere"
"she wanted to distinguish herself"
"Nunc ergo patris nostri mors erit".
"so now she will be the death of our father"
"et tamen illa non lachrymam".
"and yet she does not shed a tear"
"Quare clamo?" respondit pulchritudo

"Why should I cry?" answered Beauty
"Clamor valde supervacuus esset"
"crying would be very needless"
"Pater meus non patietur pro me".
"my father will not suffer for me"
"Monstrum unam ex filiabus accipiet"
"the monster will accept of one of his daughters"
"Omni furori suo me offeram".
"I will offer myself up to all his fury"
"Ego sum gauisus, quia mors mea animam patris mei saluabit".
"I am very happy, because my death will save my father's life"
"Mors mea documentum erit amoris mei"
"my death will be a proof of my love"
"Minime, soror," dixit ei tres fratres
"No, sister," said her three brothers
"quod non erit"
"that shall not be"
"Ibimus invenire monstrum"
"we will go find the monster"
"et aut occidemus eum.
"and either we will kill him..."
"... vel in conatu peribimus".
"... or we will perish in the attempt"
"Nolite, filii mei," dixit mercator
"Do not imagine any such thing, my sons," said the merchant
" Tanta est bestiae potestas ut eum nulla spe superare posses ".
"the Beast's power is so great that I have no hope you could overcome him"
"Delectatus sum specie et liberalitate";
"I am charmed with Beauty's kind and generous offer"
"sed liberalitatem accipere non possum".
"but I cannot accept to her generosity"
"Senex sum, et non diu vivere"
"I am old, and I don't have long to live"

"Sic paucis annis possum solvere"
"so I can only loose a few years"
"Tempus quod paenitet vos, filii carissimi"
"time which I regret for you, my dear children"
"Sed pater," inquit, "pulchritudo"
"But father," said Beauty
"non ad palatium sine me".
"you shall not go to the palace without me"
"Non potes prohibere me ab his te"
"you cannot stop me from following you"
nihil aliud potest arguere pulchritudinem
nothing could convince Beauty otherwise
institit ad bysso regis
she insisted on going to the fine palace
et sorores eius delectabantur instantiae
and her sisters were delighted at her insistence

Mercator anxius erat cogitationem amittendi filiam
The merchant was worried at the thought of losing his daughter
in tantum sollicitus erat ut de pectore pleno aureo oblitus esset
he was so worried that he had forgotten about the chest full of gold
noctu ad quietem se contulit, et cubiculi sui ianuam clausit
at night he retired to rest, and he shut his chamber door
deinde, cum magna admiratione, thesaurum invenit in lecto suo
then, to his great astonishment, he found the treasure by his bedside
voluit dicere liberos
he was determined not to tell his children
si scirent, se in oppidum reverti voluisse
if they knew, they would have wanted to return to town
et placuit ne excederet agris
and he was resolved not to leave the countryside

sed secreto speravit decorem
but he trusted Beauty with the secret
nuntiavit duos viros venisse
she informed him that two gentlemen had came
et rogaverunt eam
and they made proposals to her sisters
orabatque patrem, ut consentiret in matrimonium
she begged her father to consent to their marriage
et petiit ab eo ut daret eis aliquid de fortuna sua
and she asked him to give them some of his fortune
quae iam dimiserat illis
she had already forgiven them
impii linivit oculos cepis
the wicked creatures rubbed their eyes with onions
aliquas lacrimas opprimere cum sorore sua
to force some tears when they parted with their sister
sed fratres eius vere interfuerant
but her brothers really were concerned
forma solus non lacrimas
Beauty was the only one who did not shed any tears
noluit augere molestiam
she did not want to increase their uneasiness
Equo autem recto itinere ad palatium
the horse took the direct road to the palace
et ad vesperam viderunt palatium illuminatum
and towards evening they saw the illuminated palace
equus in stabulum iterum se contulit
the horse took himself into the stable again
Ingressus est autem vir bonus et filia eius in aulam magnam
and the good man and his daughter went into the great hall
hic invenerunt mensam splendide ministrantem
here they found a table splendidly served up
mercator non appetitus edendi
the merchant had no appetite to eat
forma autem hilaris videri conatus est
but Beauty endeavoured to appear cheerful

sedit ad mensam et adiuvit patrem suum
she sat down at the table and helped her father
sed et ipsa sibi;
but she also thought to herself:
"Profecto bestia me saginare vult priusquam me comedat".
"Beast surely wants to fatten me before he eats me"
"propterea quod tam copiosam oblectationem praebet".
"that is why he provides such plentiful entertainment"
postquam comederunt clamorem magnum audiverunt
after they had eaten they heard a great noise
et miserum puerum suum cum lacrimis in oculis suis valere iubeat
and the merchant bid his unfortunate child farewell, with tears in his eyes
quia sciebat venire bestiam
because he knew the Beast was coming
forma horrenda formidinis
Beauty was terrified at his horrid form
sed accepit animum quantum poterat
but she took courage as well as she could
et interrogavit eam monstrum si volens veniret
and the monster asked her if she came willingly
"Libenter veni", inquit tremens
"yes, I have come willingly," she said trembling
Respondit bestia : Valde bona es.
the Beast responded, "You are very good"
"Et ego vehementer gratum tibi, honestus"
"and I am greatly obliged to you; honest man"
"Ite vias vestras cras mane"
"go your ways tomorrow morning"
"Sed numquam cogito huc iterum venire"
"but never think of coming here again"
"Vale forma, vale bestia"
"Farewell Beauty, farewell Beast," he answered
et statim monstrum recessit
and immediately the monster withdrew

"O filia," inquit mercator
"Oh, daughter," said the merchant
et iterum filiam suam amplexatus est
and he embraced his daughter once more
"Paene exterritus sum usque ad mortem"
"I am almost frightened to death"
"Crede mihi, melius fuerat redire"
"believe me, you had better go back"
"me hic manere, pro te"
"let me stay here, instead of you"
"Minime, pater", "forma" inquit, "obfirmato sono"
"No, father," said Beauty, in a resolute tone
"cras mane proficisceris"
"you shall set out tomorrow morning"
" meque ad providentiae curam ac tutelam relinquas " ;
"leave me to the care and protection of providence"
nihilominus cubitum ierunt
nonetheless they went to bed
Nolebant oculos claudere noctem
they thought they would not close their eyes all night
sed sicut illi dormierunt
but just as they lay down they slept

venitque mulier pulchra pulchritudine, et dixit ei:
Beauty dreamed a fine lady came and said to her:
" contentus sum, forma, voluntate tua " ;
"I am content, Beauty, with your good will"
"Hoc bonum opus tuum non irremuneratum".
"this good action of yours shall not go unrewarded"
pulchritudinem excitavit et indicavit ei patri suo somnio
Beauty waked and told her father her dream
Somnium adiuvit ut consolaretur eum paululum
the dream helped to comfort him a little
sed non potuit quin amare discederet
but he could not help crying bitterly as he was leaving

simul atque ille discessit, formositas consedit in aula magna et clamat nimis
as soon as he was gone, Beauty sat down in the great hall and cried too
sed placuit non esse sollicitam
but she resolved not to be uneasy
decrevit valere ad modicum tempus vivere reliquerat
she decided to be strong for the little time she had left to live
quia firmiter credidit bestiam manducare illam
because she firmly believed the Beast would eat her
sed etiam regiam explorare poterat
however, she thought she might as well explore the palace
et voluit videre castrum nobile
and she wanted to view the fine castle
castrum quod non admirans
a castle which she could not help admiring
amoenissimum erat palatium
it was a delightfully pleasant palace
et valde admiratus est cum vidisset ostium
and she was extremely surprised at seeing a door
et super januam scriptam esse illam cameram suam
and over the door was written that it was her room
aperiens ostium cito
she opened the door hastily
eratque ea loci magnificentia praestringebatur
and she was quite dazzled with the magnificence of the room
quae praecipue operam suam in bibliothecam grandem habebat
what chiefly took up her attention was a large library
chorda et aliquot musicae libri
a harpsichord and several music books
"Bene" dixit secum
"Well," said she to herself
"Video ne feram meam tempus gravem pendeat";
"I see the Beast will not let my time hang heavy"
tum reflectitur ad se de suo situ

then she reflected to herself about her situation
"Si maneret dies, haec omnia hic non essent"
"If I was meant to stay a day all this would not be here"
Haec ratio nova animo
this consideration inspired her with fresh courage
et sumpsit librum ex nova bibliotheca
and she took a book from her new library
et haec in aureis litteris legit;
and she read these words in golden letters:
"grata forma, pelle timorem";
"Welcome Beauty, banish fear"
"Tu es regina et domina hic"
"You are queen and mistress here"
" Loquere vota tua, loquere voluntatem tuam ".
"Speak your wishes, speak your will"
"Citis obsequium votis tuis hic obvium".
"Swift obedience meets your wishes here"
"Heu," inquit, cum gemitu
"Alas," said she, with a sigh
"Maxime pauperem patrem meum videre cupio".
"Most of all I wish to see my poor father"
"Et volo scire quid sit facere"
"and I would like to know what he is doing"
Haec ubi dixisset, speculum animadvertit
As soon as she had said this she noticed the mirror
ingenti admiratione sui vidit domum suam in speculo
to her great amazement she saw her own home in the mirror
pater eius venit in passione existens fessus
her father arrived emotionally exhausted
sororibus eius in occursum eius
her sisters went to meet him
non obstante conatu moesti apparere, gaudium eorum apparebat
despite their attempts to appear sorrowful, their joy was visible
momento post omnia evanuerunt

a moment later everything disappeared
et pulchritudinis apprehensio disparuit nimis
and Beauty's apprehensions disappeared too
sciebat enim se posse confidere bestiae
for she knew she could trust the Beast

In meridie cenam paratam invenit
At noon she found dinner ready
et sedit ad mensam
she sat herself down at the table
et excepta concentu musicorum
and she was entertained with a concert of music
quamvis non viderent aliorum
although she couldn't see anybody
nocte iterum consedit ad cenam
at night she sat down for supper again
hoc tempore audivit vocem bestiae factae
this time she heard the noise the Beast made
et non poterat perterritus
and she could not help being terrified
"pulchritudo" dixit monstrum
"Beauty," said the monster
"Nonne sinitis me vobiscum manducare?"
"do you allow me to eat with you?"
"facies ut lubet", formidolosa respondit pulchritudo
"do as you please," Beauty answered trembling
"Non," respondit bestia
"No," replied the Beast
"Tu solus domina es hic"
"you alone are mistress here"
"Potes me mittere, si molestum sum"
"you can send me away if I'm troublesome"
"Mitte me et statim recedere"
"send me away and I will immediately withdraw"
"Sed dic mihi, nonne me turpissimum putas?"
"But, tell me; do you not think I am very ugly?"

"Verum est," inquit, pulchritudinem
"That is true," said Beauty
"Non possum dicere mendacium"
"I cannot tell a lie"
"Sed credo te valde benignum"
"but I believe you are very good natured"
"Immo ego sum" dixit monstrum
"I am indeed," said the monster
"Sed sine deformitate, ego quoque nihil sum".
"But apart from my ugliness, I also have no sense"
"Scio me ipsum stultam esse creaturam".
"I know very well that I am a silly creature"
"Non est signum stultitiae ita cogitare," respondit pulchritudo
"It is no sign of folly to think so," replied Beauty
"ede igitur, forma," dixit monstrum
"Eat then, Beauty," said the monster
"Conare ludere in palatio tuo"
"try to amuse yourself in your palace"
"Omnia hic tua sunt"
"everything here is yours"
"Et ego valde anxius essem si non esses beatus"
"and I would be very uneasy if you were not happy"
"Pergratum es" respondit pulchritudinem
"You are very obliging," answered Beauty
" Fateor, benignitate tua delector"
"I admit I am pleased with your kindness"
"et cum tuam humanitatem considero, turpitudines tuas vix considero".
"and when I consider your kindness, I hardly notice your deformities"
"Est," inquit bestia, "bonum est cor meum."
"Yes, yes," said the Beast, "my heart is good
"sed quamvis bonus sum, monstrum tamen sum".
"but although I am good, I am still a monster"
"Multi sunt viri qui hoc nomine meruerunt plus quam tu";

"There are many men that deserve that name more than you"
"et malo tibi sicut tu es"
"and I prefer you just as you are"
"et malo tibi plus quam eos qui ingratum cor abscondunt".
"and I prefer you more than those who hide an ungrateful heart"
"si modo aliquem sensum haberem," respondit bestia
"if only I had some sense," replied the Beast
"Si sensissem, bene gratias agerem"
"if I had sense I would make a fine compliment to thank you"
"At ego tam hebes"
"but I am so dull"
"Nisi possum dicere, tibi sum valde gratum"
"I can only say I am greatly obliged to you"
pulchritudinem comedit cenam
Beauty ate a hearty supper
et prope terrorem monstri vicerat
and she had almost conquered her dread of the monster
sed deficere volebat, cum bestiam sibi proximam quaereret
but she wanted to faint when the Beast asked her the next question
"pulchritudo eris uxor?"
"Beauty, will you be my wife?"
tulit aliquanto ante posset respondere
she took some time before she could answer
quia timebat ne irascatur
because she was afraid of making him angry
tandem tamen "nequaquam," inquit, "bestia".
at last, however, she said "no, Beast"
monstrum pauperis statim exsibilatur vehementer
immediately the poor monster hissed very frightfully
et totum palatium resonabat
and the whole palace echoed
sed pulchritudo mox a pavore convaluit
but Beauty soon recovered from her fright
quia bestia iterum flebili voce locutus est

because Beast spoke again in a mournful voice
"Vale igitur, pulchritudo".
"then farewell, Beauty"
et solus reversus interdum
and he only turned back now and then
ut exiens intueri illam
to look at her as he went out

Nunc autem sola pulchritudo
now Beauty was alone again
plurimum misericordia sensit
she felt a great deal of compassion
"Ei, mille piae sunt!"
"Alas, it is a thousand pities"
"Nihil tam ingeniosum neque tam turpe".
"anything so good natured should not be so ugly"
pulchritudinis tres menses in palatio valde contente consumpsit
Beauty spent three months very contentedly in the palace
omne vespere bestia pretium eius a visit
every evening the Beast paid her a visit
et loquebatur in cena
and they talked during supper
ipsi loquebatur cum sensu communi
they talked with common sense
sed non loqui quod vocant testimonium
but they didn't talk with what people call wittiness
forma semper aliquid pretiosum in bestia
Beauty always discovered some valuable character in the Beast
et adsueverat deformitatem suam
and she had gotten used to his deformity
et non pertimesco tempus visitationis suae amplius
she didn't dread the time of his visit anymore
saepe iam vigilavit ad eam
now she often looked at her watch

et non poterat expectare horam nonam
and she couldn't wait for it to be nine o'clock
quia numquam bestiam illam horam exciderunt
because the Beast never missed coming at that hour
una res ad pulchritudinem
there was only one thing that concerned Beauty
tota nocte antequam cubitum irent, bestia eandem quaestionem interrogabat
every night before she went to bed the Beast asked her the same question
monstrum interrogavit eam si esset uxor eius
the monster asked her if she would be his wife
dixitque ad eum quadam die, " Bestia, turbata est mihi valde ";
one day she said to him, "Beast, you make me very uneasy"
"Vellem possem consentire in uxorem ducere"
"I wish I could consent to marry you"
"sed nimis sincerus sum ut credas me nubere te"
"but I am too sincere to make you believe I would marry you"
"Matrimonium nostrum numquam fiet"
"our marriage will never happen"
"Ego te ut amicus semper videbo"
"I shall always see you as a friend"
"Quaeso experiri satiari"
"please try to be satisfied with this"
"Satiari oportet hoc," inquit bestia
"I must be satisfied with this," said the Beast
"Scio me infortunium";
"I know my own misfortune"
"sed te amo summa affectione "
"but I love you with the tenderest affection"
"Sed me beatum debere existimare".
"However, I ought to consider myself as happy"
"et me beatum esse ut hic maneas".
"and I should be happy that you will stay here"
"Promittere me numquam me relinquere"

"promise me never to leave me"
pulchritudo erubuit his verbis
Beauty blushed at these words

unus dies pulchritudo est vultus in speculo
one day Beauty was looking in her mirror
pater suus anxius erat sibi male pro ea
her father had worried himself sick for her
adhuc plus quam semper videre cupiebat
she longed to see him again more than ever
"Possum polliceri numquam te totum relinquere"
"I could promise never to leave you entirely"
"sed desiderii est videre patrem meum".
"but I have so great a desire to see my father"
"Impossibiliter commotus essem si negas"
"I would be impossibly upset if you say no"
'monstrum' inquit 'malo me mori'
"I had rather die myself," said the monster
"Malo mori quam te turbat".
"I would rather die than make you feel uneasiness"
"Mittam te ad patrem tuum".
"I will send you to your father"
"cum eo manebitis".
"you shall remain with him"
"et misera haec bestia pro moerore morietur".
"and this unfortunate Beast will die with grief instead"
"Minime", inquit decor, flens
"No," said Beauty, weeping
" Nimium te amo ut mortis tuae causa sit ".
"I love you too much to be the cause of your death"
"Promissum tibi do ut per hebdomadam redeam"
"I give you my promise to return in a week"
"Monstrasti mihi sorores meae nuptae".
"You have shown me that my sisters are married"
"et fratres mei iverunt ad exercitum".
"and my brothers have gone to the army"

"Sine septimana cum patre meo, sicut solus est".
"let me stay a week with my father, as he is alone"
"Eris ibi cras mane," dixit bestia
"You shall be there tomorrow morning," said the Beast
"sed memor promissionis tuae"
"but remember your promise"
"Tu tantum debes anulum tuum in mensa ponere antequam cubitum ambules"
"You need only lay your ring on a table before you go to bed"
"et tunc mane redieris".
"and then you will be brought back before the morning"
" Vale cara pulchritudo " ingemuit bestia
"Farewell dear Beauty," sighed the Beast
forma cubitum ibat tristissima nocte
Beauty went to bed very sad that night
quia noluit videre bestia tam sollicitus
because she didn't want to see Beast so worried

Postridie mane invenit se in domo patris sui
the next morning she found herself at her father's home
et pulsavit campanulam a lecto
she rung a little bell by her bedside
et ancilla magna voce
and the maid gave a loud shriek
et pater susum cucurrit
and her father ran upstairs
putabat se cum gaudio moriturum
he thought he was going to die with joy
tenebat in armis ad quartam horam
he held her in his arms for quarter of an hour
Tandem prima salutatio praefecti
eventually the first greetings were over
forma coepit cogitare de lecto
Beauty began to think of getting out of bed
sed cognovit se non induisse
but she realized she had brought no clothes

sed ancilla ei se invenisse pyxidem dixit
but the maid told her she had found a box
truncus magnus erat plenus togis et coquit
the large trunk was full of gowns and dresses
unaquaque toga erat auro et adamantibus
each gown was covered with gold and diamonds
forma gratias bestias pro huiusmodi cura
Beauty thanked Beast for his kind care
et tulit unam de planissimis vestimentis
and she took one of the plainest of the dresses
dare se intendebat ad alias vestes sororibus
she intended to give the other dresses to her sisters
sed in eo pectore vestes evanuerunt
but at that thought the chest of clothes disappeared
bestia institerat vestimenta sua solum
Beast had insisted the clothes were for her only
pater ei quod ita esset
her father told her that this was the case
et statim truncus vestimentorum reversus est
and immediately the trunk of clothes came back again
pulchritudo induit se novis vestibus
Beauty dressed herself with her new clothes
et interea ancillis ierunt ut sorores suas invenirent
and in the meantime maids went to find her sisters
et soror eius cum viris
both her sister were with their husbands
sed et sorores eius erant valde infelices
but both her sisters were very unhappy
soror eius primogenita duxerat pulcherrimum virum
her eldest sister had married a very handsome gentleman
sed adeo cupidus fuit ut uxorem neglexisset
but he was so fond of himself that he neglected his wife
ea secunda soror duxerat homo lepidus
her second sister had married a witty man
sed utebatur testi- monio suo ad torquendum populum
but he used his wittiness to torment people

et uxorem suam maxime cruciabat
and he tormented his wife most of all
pulchritudinis sororibus vidit eam ornatu princeps
Beauty's sisters saw her dressed like a princess
et ægrotabantur zelo
and they were sickened with envy
nunc fuit pulchrior umquam
now she was more beautiful than ever
eam affectuosas mores ne extinguant invidiam
her affectionate behaviour could not stifle their jealousy
dixit eis quomodo beatus esset cum bestia
she told them how happy she was with the Beast
et zelus eorum paratus erat ad erumpendum
and their jealousy was ready to burst

et descenderunt in hortum, ut clamarent de calamitate sua
They went down into the garden to cry about their misfortune
"Quomodo est haec creatura melior nobis?"
"In what way is this little creature better than us?"
"Quare debet esse tanto beatior?"
"Why should she be so much happier?"
"Soror" dixit maior soror
"Sister," said the older sister
"Cogitaverunt iustus percussit animam meam"
"a thought just struck my mind"
"conemur eam hic plus quam hebdomade retinere"
"let us try to keep her here for more than a week"
"Facebit fortasse hoc monstrum stultum".
"perhaps this will enrage the silly monster"
"quia verbum rupisset"
"because she would have broken her word"
"et tunc devoraret eam";
"and then he might devour her"
"id est magna idea," respondit altera soror
"that's a great idea," answered the other sister
"Debemus illam quam maxime misericordiam"

"we must show her as much kindness as possible"
Hanc fecerunt sorores
the sisters made this their resolution
et sorori suae amantissime agebant
and they behaved very affectionately to their sister
forma pauperis flebat gaudium ab omni bonitate sua
poor Beauty wept for joy from all their kindness
Cum autem completa esset dies, clamaverunt et sciderunt comam suam
when the week was expired, they cried and tore their hair
videbantur ita paenitet ad partem eius
they seemed so sorry to part with her
et pulchritudinis promissam manere hebdomadam
and Beauty promised to stay a week longer

Interea, pulchritudo in se ipsam reflectere non potuit
In the meantime, Beauty could not help reflecting on herself
anxius quid ageret ad bestiam pauperem
she worried what she was doing to poor Beast
se scire se sincere dilexit eum
she know that she sincerely loved him
et vere desiderabat videre illum
and she really longed to see him again
decima nocte pergit ad patris nimis
the tenth night she spent at her father's too
vidit eam in horto palatio
she dreamed she was in the palace garden
et vidit in gramine bestiam
and she dreamt she saw the Beast extended on the grass
obicere eam vocem morientis videbatur
he seemed to reproach her in a dying voice
et de ingratitudine accusavit eam
and he accused her of ingratitude
pulchritudinem experrectus a somno
Beauty woke up from her sleep
et in lacrimas

and she burst into tears

"Nonne nimis impius sum?"
"Am I not very wicked?"
"Nonne me crudelis tam inclementer facere ad bestiam?"
"Was it not cruel of me to act so unkindly to the Beast?"
"Bestia omnia mihi placebat"
"Beast did everything to please me"
"Numquid tam turpe est ut eius culpa sit?"
"Is it his fault that he is so ugly?"
"Numquid tam parum ingenii culpa est?"
"Is it his fault that he has so little wit?"
" benignus est et bonus, et satis est ";
"He is kind and good, and that is sufficient"
"Cur non negavi uxorem ducere?"
"Why did I refuse to marry him?"
"me beatum esse cum monstro"
"I should be happy with the monster"
"Aspice viros sororum mearum"
"look at the husbands of my sisters"
"Neque testis eos bonos neque pulcher facit".
"neither wittiness, nor a being handsome makes them good"
"Neque maritos suos beatos facit".
"neither of their husbands makes them happy"
sed virtus, suavitas ingenii et patientiae.
"but virtue, sweetness of temper, and patience"
"Haec faciunt femina felix"
"these things make a woman happy"
"et belua has omnes pretiosas qualitates habet".
"and the Beast has all these valuable qualities"
"Verum est; viscera erga illum non sentio"
"it is true; I do not feel the tenderness of affection for him"
"sed habeo maximam gratiam pro eo".
"but I find I have the highest gratitude for him"
"et habeo maximam gratiam in eo"
"and I have the highest esteem of him"
"Et ipse est amicus meus optimus"

"and he is my best friend"
"Miserum illum non faciam"
"I will not make him miserable"
"Si tam ingratus essem, numquam mihi ignoscerem".
"If were I to be so ungrateful I would never forgive myself"
pulchritudo posuit eam anulum in mensa
Beauty put her ring on the table
et iterum ad lectum
and she went to bed again
vix erat in lecto priusquam obdormivit
scarce was she in bed before she fell asleep

et iterum mane experrectus
she woke up again the next morning
et laetabatur se in palatio bestiae invenire
and she was overjoyed to find herself in the Beast's palace
induit unum ex veste nicest ut placeat ei
she put on one of her nicest dress to please him
et patientiam expectabat ad vesperam
and she patiently waited for evening
venit hora exoptata
at last the wished-for hour came
hora percussit horologium, nulla tamen bestia apparuit
the clock struck nine, yet no Beast appeared
formi- tum timuit leti causa fuisse
Beauty then feared she had been the cause of his death
et cucurrit clamor in circuitu regis
she ran crying all around the palace
cum ubique quaereret , recordata est somnii sui
after having sought for him everywhere, she remembered her dream
et cucurrit ad canalem in horto
and she ran to the canal in the garden
Ibi invenit bestia pauperem extenta
there she found poor Beast stretched out
et certe occiderat

and she was sure she had killed him
se ei sine ullo terrore projecit
she threw herself upon him without any dread
cor ejus adhuc verberans
his heart was still beating
et aquam de canali
she fetched some water from the canal
et effudit aquam super caput eius
and she poured the water on his head
Aperiens bestia oculos et locutus est ad pulchritudinem
the Beast opened his eyes and spoke to Beauty
"Promissionis tuae oblitus es"
"You forgot your promise"
"Tanta sum animo amisisse te"
"I was so heartbroken to have lost you"
"Destinavi me fame";
"I resolved to starve myself"
"Sed habeo felicitatem videndi te semel"
"but I have the happiness of seeing you once more"
" sic mihi placet mori satur " ;
"so I have the pleasure of dying satisfied"
"Minime, cara bestia," dixit forma, "non morieris";
"No, dear Beast," said Beauty, "you must not die"
"Vivat ut sit vir meus"
"Live to be my husband"
"Ex hoc tempore manum meam do tibi"
"from this moment I give you my hand"
et iuro non esse nisi tuum.
"and I swear to be none but yours"
"Heu! Ego tantum amicitiam tibi cogitavi"
"Alas! I thought I had only a friendship for you"
sed dolor, quem nunc sentio, arguit;
"but the grief I now feel convinces me;"
"Non possum vivere nec sine te"
"I cannot live without you"
vix haec dixerat pulchritudo, cum vidit lucem

Beauty scarce had said these words when she saw a light
palatium micans lux
the palace sparkled with light
pompa caelum inluminavit
fireworks lit up the sky
et aerem repleti musicis
and the air filled with music
omnia denuntiavit magno eventu
everything gave notice of some great event
sed nihil potuit eam attendere
but nothing could hold her attention
et convertit ad eam cari bestia
she turned to her dear Beast
bestia cui tremuit
the Beast for whom she trembled with fear
sed admiratio magna ex eo quod vidit.
but her surprise was great at what she saw!
bestia abiit
the Beast had disappeared
loco vidit pulcherrimum princeps
instead she saw the loveliest prince
quae finem habuit alica
she had put an end to the spell
incantamentum quo ad similitudinem bestiae
a spell under which he resembled a Beast
hic princeps omni attentione dignus erat
this prince was worthy of all her attention
sed non poterat non quaerere ubi esset bestia
but she could not help but ask where the Beast was
"Vides eum ante pedes tuos", dixit princeps
"You see him at your feet," said the prince
"Improbus mediocris damnavit me"
"A wicked fairy had condemned me"
"Ego in illa figura manerem donec pulcherrima regina me nubere consensit"

"I was to remain in that shape until a beautiful princess agreed to marry me"
"Infandi absconderunt intellectum meum"
"the fairy hid my understanding"
"Unicus eras satis liberalis, ut amoenitatem ingenii mei bonitate"
"you were the only one generous enough to be charmed by the goodness of my temper"
pulchritudo feliciter oppressit
Beauty was happily surprised
et dedit manum lepidi principi suo
and she gave the charming prince her hand
venerunt in castra
they went together into the castle
et delectatus est decor invenire patrem in arce
and Beauty was overjoyed to find her father in the castle
et tota familia eius ibi erant
and her whole family were there too
etiam pulchra domina, quae in somnio apparuit ibi
even the beautiful lady that appeared in her dream was there
"pulchritudo" dixit domina ex somnio
"Beauty," said the lady from the dream
"Veni et accipe mercedem tuam".
"come and receive your reward"
" Virtutem ingenio vel vultu praetulisti "
"you have preferred virtue over wit or looks"
"et merearis aliquem, in quo talia uniuntur".
"and you deserve someone in whom these qualities are united"
"Tu es futurus regina magna"
"you are going to be a great queen"
" Spero thronum virtutis tuae non minuet "
"I hope the throne will not lessen your virtue"
deinde mediocris ad duas sorores
then the fairy turned to the two sisters
"Vidi intra corda vestra"

"I have seen inside your hearts"
"et scio omnem malitiam continent corda vestra"
"and I know all the malice your hearts contain"
"tu duo signa fient"
"you two will become statues"
"sed animum vestrum servabitis"
"but you will keep your minds"
stabis ad portas palatii sororis tuae.
"you shall stand at the gates of your sister's palace"
" Felicitas sororis tuae poena tua erit "
"your sister's happiness shall be your punishment"
"Non poteris redire ad statum pristinum"
"you won't be able to return to your former states"
"Nisi vitia vestra faterimini".
"unless, you both admit your faults"
"sed praevideo vos statuas semper manere".
"but I am foresee that you will always remain statues"
"Superbia, ira, gula, atque otium vincuntur".
"pride, anger, gluttony, and idleness are sometimes conquered"
" invidorum autem et malignorum mentium miracula sunt conversio "
"but the conversion of envious and malicious minds are miracles"
statim mediocris dedit ictum cum virga
immediately the fairy gave a stroke with her wand
et subito deportati sunt omnes, qui erant in atrio
and in a moment all that were in the hall were transported
ierant in principatus principis
they had gone into the prince's dominions
principis subditi eum gaudio receperunt
the prince's subjects received him with joy
sacerdos accepit pulchritudinem et bestia
the priest married Beauty and the Beast
et vixit cum ea multis annis
and he lived with her many years

et felicitas perfecta
and their happiness was complete
quia felicitas eorum in virtute fundata est
because their happiness was founded on virtue

Finis
The End

www.ingramcontent.com/pod-product-compliance
Lightning Source LLC
Chambersburg PA
CBHW012013090526
44590CB00026B/3991